Secrets & Lies

What Happened Next

Belinda Conniss

Secrets & Lies

The sequel to *Sad, Lonely & A Long Way From Home*

A continuation of my life back in Scotland

Although this book is based on true events, the names and some of the places have been changed, to protect the identities of some of the people mentioned.

Contents

Introduction

Secrets & Lies is the sequel to *Sad Lonely & A Long Way From Home.* It continues with my life back in Scotland, the good, the bad and the downright ugly.

'The good' being married to a wonderful man, and having three beautiful daughters and three wonderful grandchildren.

'The bad' being secrets and lies, the things that were kept from me for all those years which broke my heart.

'The ugly' being the things that have hurt me this last seventeen years.

Back In Scotland

It was hard coming to terms with the fact that I was back in Scotland for good this time, even though I was in contact with my daughter, Leanne, more than when I was living in Wales, but that didn't really last long.

Her stepmother tried to put a stop to us being together on several occasions which pretty much left me in tears a lot of the time. Then came the time that she told me she didn't want to see me for a while, I shed tears every day for a long, long time.

Looking back, I don't blame Leanne for that decision, but I will never forgive her stepmother for her involvement. It all happened so fast; I was in the local bus station with my sister who happened to notice Leanne across the way, hiding behind her stepmother. She thought that I couldn't see her – but I did!

Sadly, I had those familiar, horrible feelings in my tummy, and the sadness of wondering why Leanne would hide from her own mother, made me feel physically sick. I didn't go to her or call her name, instead, I waited until I got home to my mother's and I called her.

I was staying with my mother and father at the time because I was on the housing waiting list which was a nightmare. Being that I was on my own, I had been told that it may take some time to house me, so I slept on my parents' sofa for a while.

When I called to talk to Leanne, her dad answered the phone and said that she didn't want to speak to me. As per usual, he spoke to me in that 'bad ass' manner and attitude which told me that his partner was there.

It's the only time he spoke to me like that; when she wasn't around he couldn't be any nicer if he tried.

However, he said that our daughter didn't feel it was right to be around me for a while yet. He gave me no explanation, but deep down I knew the reason *(her stepmother)*. We had an almighty row on the phone and that was the last I heard from Leanne until she was around seventeen.

She was thirteen when she stopped seeing me, and four years is a long time not to have my daughter around me or to speak to her. No matter how I tried, it just wasn't going to happen.

I started working at the local hospital and tried to put in as many hours as I could, in order to avoid having too much time to think about Leanne, because every time I did I would cry and start feeling sick to the pit of my stomach.

I didn't want to go down the route of losing any more weight. I already only weighed just under eight stone, which was a huge achievement for me considering I came back from Wales less than seven stone, and I didn't want to start drinking again, it may not have been so easy to give up this time.

I couldn't take sleeping on my parents' sofa for much longer so one of my sisters offered to let me live in her flat while I waited to get my own place. I stayed there for several months and, although I had a job, I was still looking for other work because I planned to move overseas away from everything that made me miserable.

I carried on working and, from time to time, I still visited Wales. I needed that much because, if I didn't, Lord only knows where I would have ended up.

Before, when I moved back to Wales for the second time, I had worked in a frozen food factory for a while and made some amazing friends who helped me through a lot.

Every time I went to Wales I still made a point of visiting them and staying over at their homes too. I will forever be in their debt for being so kind to me.

One of my closest friends, Neville, *(God rest him)* was the kindest and sweetest friend ever. I think, looking back, I saw him as a kind of father figure. We worked together and I stayed with him on my visits. We had many a night out with other friends, he really was the best. I miss Neville dearly and think of him often. He was sixty-five when he passed away and, by this time, I had been back in Scotland for ten years. I will never forget how sad I was on that day.

The month before Neville passed away, I was in Wales for my friend Pam's, father's funeral, which was also a shock as he wasn't an ill man. He always seemed to manage getting around okay and then that dreadful day came and he had passed away.

On the day of the funeral, Neville took me to the Crematorium then went back home to wait for me as I was going on to the wake.

I remember saying to Neville the day before I left to go back home, I don't know what I would do if anything happened to you. He said, "I wish I was coming up to Scotland with you. I could do with the break."

I replied, "Pack your case and come."

He had been feeling down for a while because he wasn't too well, but he said no to me because it was too short notice.

"Maybe I will pack a few things and come next week," he said. I was pleased because he had been to stay a few times previously.

A couple of weeks later, Neville's daughter called me to say he was in hospital, very ill, and she wasn't sure if he was going to make it. I can't remember how many days after, as it's pretty much a blur, but I will never forget receiving the call to tell me that he had passed away.

I was broken-hearted, and my husband came down with me for the funeral; it was a very sad day. I had become friends with Neville's daughter and son-in-law before he passed away, and I remember her asking me before the funeral if I wanted to go and see him.

He was in his coffin at his house, but I just couldn't do it. I had seen my grandmother *(my stepdad's mum)*, when I was fourteen, in her coffin and swore I would never look at another dead person again.

I was with my grandmother when she passed away of a heart attack. It's not something I ever want to see again and it was the first time I had seen a man cry. My grandfather had sat there holding her hand as she slipped away.

My mother took me to go see my grandmother in her coffin and said I had to kiss her forehead but, as I bent down to do so, I froze. I just couldn't and ran out the room crying, *(apparently I had nightmares for a few weeks afterwards, although I can't remember this)* and I wasn't allowed to go to her funeral.

In fact, the first time I saw my grandmother's grave was when we buried my grandfather *(her husband)* which was twenty-four years later. I have never been since. *Shame on me!*

By now, I had given up my job at the hospital because I had found a job in a travel agent in Edinburgh which I loved. I've always had good knowledge when it comes to other countries because of all the travelling I have done.

I moved out of my sister's flat because we started having the odd row *(nothing new)*. It was a constant thing with her and me when we were younger. My youngest sister moved up to the north of Scotland so I rented her house until I could get my own home.

It was the night before my birthday and my sisters talked me into going out for the evening to celebrate. I wasn't really one for going out but I thought, *Okay let's go, I need to let my hair down and relax.*

I'm really glad that we went out that night. I was standing at the bar chatting away and I heard a voice say to me, "Belinda, can you pass me that ashtray?"

I reached for the ashtray and went to pass it to the voice behind me only to recognise the face.

"Oh my God," I said, "I know you; we went to high school together right?"

The man said, "Yes, we did, but can you remember my name?"

I had to think for a minute and then I replied, "It's Jerry."

He nodded and asked, "Can you remember my surname?" To my shame, I couldn't. However, Jerry did tell me after.

He asked how I was and what I had been up too as we hadn't seen each other in around fifteen years. So, of course, we got chatting and I told him that I had lived in Wales for quite a few years but had now come back to Scotland.

Jerry said that he had seen me in the pub a couple of times but didn't want to come over and speak to me, as I was with other people, which was true. I used to finish my shift on a Thursday and Friday and pop in there for a Cola before heading home.

He asked what I was up too after the pub and I told him that we were going on to a nightclub. I wasn't working the next day so why not? It was also my birthday the following day, so I might as well enjoy myself.

Jerry said to me, "If I go home and get changed [he was in his working clothes] and come to the nightclub will you give me a dance?"

"Of course I will," I said with a little excitement! I knew Jerry from when we were in high school at the age of thirteen and, yes, I did like him but never approached him because he hung around with those I would describe as 'popular' and he also had a girlfriend.

About two hours later, we were in the nightclub and I kept watching the door to see if Jerry would come walking in and each time the door opened it wasn't him, then, eventually, there he was.

So, there was I with those old familiar feelings in my tummy again. I didn't see any harm as there was nobody else to think about and, *if* I was to see someone, I wasn't planning to settle down again.

We had a great night dancing, laughing and just enjoying each other's company and, for the first time in a long while, I was happy again.

By this time, my sisters were off dancing with each other and I hoped that they wouldn't think I had ditched them but, truthfully, I think deep down they were happy to leave me to it because they knew how miserable I had been over the past few months.

The night finally came to an end and I was quite tipsy, to say the least, and so was Jerry. He asked if he could take me home and, of course, I said yes. We chatted for a long time. I told him a little about myself and how I had ended up in Wales, then back to Scotland. Although I had known Jerry for many years, I didn't go into too much detail.

I explained that I was married and waiting for a divorce. He told me that he had split from his long-term partner a few months earlier.

I can't remember what time it was, but I know it was the early hours of the morning. I had known Jerry for so long; it was lovely just to have someone I could relate to.

The fact that we had both gone through similar heartbreak meant that we understood one another and how it felt to be let down.

Jerry has worked all his adult life and never taken a day off work except for annual leave, yet he called in the next day to say that he was sick. He wanted to spend the day with me and, yes, I enjoyed it. We agreed to meet again in the pub that night.

2
The Divorce

I remember a friend saying to me, "When you get your divorce we will go out and celebrate."

"Celebrate," I said, "Why would I want to do that?"

"Are you kidding?" she replied, "everyone celebrates when they get divorced because they are free."

"Well," I said, "I don't think that's something to celebrate. After all, we did love each other once."

It was September 1997 when I received the letter with my Decree Nisei telling me that we were divorced as of 2nd July, 1997.

I sat there, looking at the papers, remembering what my friend said about celebrating and broke down in tears. We had been married for almost six years. I had loved that man so much and this is what it had come too. It most definitely wasn't something to celebrate.

Looking back now, I'm not sure if maybe, *just maybe,* if he had asked me to go back again, I might have thought about it. I'm glad, though, that wasn't the case because Jerry and I had been getting along just fine.

I had previously applied for two jobs overseas, one was in Portugal, selling timeshare properties, and the other was in Germany in the Navy working as a secretary. And guess what? I was offered both jobs, so now I had the dilemma of trying to figure out which one I was going to take – and how I was going to tell Jerry!

Jerry and I had been seeing each for a few months by then, and Leanne wasn't in my life. It wasn't long after that Jerry and I were in his mum's house, just chatting, when Jerry said to me that he had feelings for me. My immediate thought was *What do I do now?*

I did like Jerry very much and I did care for him, but what about the job offers? I was excited when I was offered both positions, it was my chance to start all over again where nobody knew me and didn't need to know anything about me either. It was something I always wanted to do, live overseas.

I had to be honest with Jerry about the job offers. He said that if I wanted to take up one of the offers and move away he would understand. I asked him three questions: "Have you ever cheated on a woman? Have you ever hit a woman? Do you have a temper?" Silly, I know, but after what I had been through I was too scared to fall for anyone again.

He answered, "No, not at all, I've never hit a woman and I've never cheated. Yes, I like a drink at the end of a working week, like most men, but I don't stay out all night and come home pissed and start an argument."

That was it then; I had my answers, so I turned down both jobs and decided I would give it a go with Jerry.

I did have some reservations but, because I had known Jerry all those years, just maybe, I should give him the benefit of the doubt.

For the next few months we both worked, seeing each other most nights and going out every weekend to our local pub. We had weekends away with friends, organised by our local pub and had a great time.

By the following year, things were moving along a step and Jerry asked me how I would feel about him moving in with me. I hadn't given myself time to think about it but I said, "Yes."

He told me that he would wait until the weekend, talk to his mum, tell her his plans and then we would move his stuff in, and that's exactly what we did. His mum was happy for him to move out of her house and in with me.

Rose *(Jerry's mum)* and I got on really well; she was a gem of a woman.

Jerry had been living with me for a couple of weeks, when it occurred to me that he had no children and I couldn't have any. Why on earth did I not tell him about this sooner? Maybe he might change his mind about us being a couple. We were both in our early thirties, he wasn't getting any younger and he must, surely, want children.

15

I came home from work one night and told him that we had to talk. From the look on his face, he must have thought either he had done something wrong or I was about to end our relationship.

That's when I told him that my ex-husband had given me an ultimatum about having to be sterilised and why. Jerry asked me if it was reversible and I said that I didn't know as I hadn't had any proper counselling beforehand.

"Well," he said, "there is only one way to find out." He asked me if I wanted more children.

"Yes, of course I do, if it's possible," I said.

I didn't expect him to be so understanding but it was a huge relief. I thought maybe I had blown it.

The next few months went by and then we went on holiday. We had Christmas and everything was going great. I made an appointment to see my doctor and explained that I had been in a relationship now for some time and we would like to have children.

I wasn't expecting him to say no!

He said that the operation would not be funded on the NHS and I would have to be treated privately, which meant he had to refer me to the Royal Infirmary in Edinburgh for a consultation to see what type of sterilisation I had had and if they could reverse it.

It turned out it was reversible but it came at a price! The consultation, the operation and the aftercare came to a total of £1,500 but, for us, the money was not a problem because to have more children would be worth every penny, no matter the cost.

First, though, I had to go and have this dye put through me to check that the operation could take place, which was a good thing, as we would have been devastated to have paid all that money for it not to work.

Jerry had to have some tests as well; to check that everything was in working order, and thankfully it was.

Before I went for this procedure they said that their success rate was 60-40 per cent that I would conceive. The Royal Infirmary in Edinburgh was the highest rate given, so that was good news on our part. We had an appointment to check my results to see if they could go ahead as planned. They said we would then wait around three months for a date to have the operation.

I sat thinking about the cost of the operation etc, and decided I was going to ask my ex-husband to fund half the cost *(stupid thinking of it now)*. But, I reasoned, that I had taken nothing from him when I left, when I was entitled to half his pension and that he would have to keep me until I married again.

I didn't want anything; no pension, no money, nothing, so yes, I would ask him to fund half the cost because he got off very lightly considering what he had done, and it wasn't fair for Jerry to have to help fund an operation that he had nothing to do with.

So, off I went to my solicitor, I told him what I wanted, he drafted the letter which was soon sent off to Peter. All I had to do was wait.

The reply I got from his solicitor was, 'Sorry, he has a partner, a mortgage and a child to keep, he can't afford to fund half the cost of your operation'. Straight to the point. *Really*, I thought, why on earth did I embarrass myself by asking in the first place?

Meanwhile, Jerry and I carried on with our lives while waiting for the hospital date. We were both very excited.

Two months later we had an appointment to go and see the hospital doctor to discuss if they would do the operation. Now we were less excited and more anxious. At the back of my mind I thought, *What happens if they say they can't do it?*

Jerry and I talked about it because I was afraid how he would feel if they said no. I quietly decided that, if the answer was no, I would end our relationship because I didn't want him going through the rest of his life without the child he always wanted.

The day came for us to visit the hospital, we were very nervous and it must have shown as I hardly said two words to Jerry, I think he knew. He said to me on our way there, "Please don't worry if they say no, I really don't mind if I can't have a child."

I didn't want to hear that as I knew, deep down, he did want a child and he would have been silently heartbroken.

We sat in the consultant's room for what seemed like a lifetime waiting, then the door opened and in she came.

"Well, I'm very pleased to tell you that we can go ahead and perform your operation. Congratulations." Jerry and I just looked at each other, then at the consultant and thanked her. By this time I was trying not to cry.

She said she would perform the operation within the next six weeks, and we both said, "Six weeks, oh my God, that is fantastic, thank you so much."

As soon as we left her room I broke down in tears. Jerry took me in his arms and hugged me tight. Well, it was a start, we just had to let nature take its course.

We left the hospital and headed into the town, Jerry said, "Let's go and have a bite to eat." Little did I know that he had already booked a table at a posh restaurant.

We sat down and ordered our drinks, then our meal. We couldn't stop talking about the future and prayed that all would come right for us both.

We sat eating our meal, which, I have to say, was beautiful, and chatting. A few minutes later a waiter came over to the table with a dozen red roses and handed them to me.

Jerry said that it didn't matter whether they could do the operation or not, he had already booked the restaurant. "It was either to cheer you up if we were rejected or celebrate if accepted because, either way, I'm not going anywhere. If the answer was no, it wouldn't have mattered to me because I love you."

The tears started again, I'm such a soppy woman I cry at the drop of a hat.

We went home and just lay in bed in each other's arms planning our future, we hadn't said anything to either of our families as we wanted the whole thing to be a surprise if, and when, I became pregnant.

A couple of weeks later, Jerry went on a night out with the boys. He used to manage a pool team so it was a regular arrangement and it never bothered me until, one night, he came home at around two-thirty in the morning.

I was, by this time, in a foul mood, as normally he would be home between twelve and twelve-thirty so you can imagine what was going through my mind, those old familiar feelings; was he cheating? Wasn't he?

We ended up rowing or, should I say, I did, Jerry just laughed and thought it was funny. And what's the worst thing any man can do to a woman when she is in a foul mood? Laugh.

Well, it just got worse and I told him, "Pack your bags in the morning it's over." Still he laughed and toddled off to bed, I was raging.

Next morning he assured me he hadn't done anything wrong. I said that I was sorry, he had an unusual smirk on his face, I just thought maybe he was just thinking how silly I was. We both set off to work.

That evening, we were getting ready to go out when Jerry came to me handed me another dozen red roses and a small box. I took it thinking it would be a pair of nice earrings.

3

Will You Marry Me?

You can imagine how elated I was when I opened the box and Jerry said, "Will you marry me?" The excitement was too much and I cried again, I kept thinking, *This is all a dream.*

First we had the good news of being able to have the reversal of my sterilisation, now this.

"Of course I will marry you," I said through my tears. Jerry smiled and took me in his arms, I felt so warm, safe and loved.

The time came for the operation, July 1998, and we were so excited, as off we went to the hospital.

Jerry waited in the hospital until it was all over and I was back in the ward. He said that I was so doped, I kept asking him to press the button for me to have more pain relief, but he wasn't allowed I had to do it myself.

He told me that I was so out of it I just kept pressing the button that, at one point, I looked up looked at all the other patients and said to him, "See them, they are all mad." Then I started talking about 'sheep dip'. Subconsciously, Wales must have been in the back of my mind.

The surgeon came to see us the next day and said that the operation had gone well but I only had one working tube as the other was blocked. I asked her what that meant. She explained that my chances of conceiving had gone from 60-40 per cent to 40-60 per cent.

Boy was that a shock, still, we had to remain positive and leave it in God's hands.

A couple of months earlier we had booked a holiday to Portugal, six weeks after the operation as that's how long I needed to recover.

The holiday in Portugal was so relaxing for us both, after coping with work and the stress of the forthcoming operation, hoping that all would turn out right.

Then, it was back home and back to work. One day, shortly after, I wasn't feeling too good. I had this nauseous feeling accompanied with a bad back, although the bad back was nothing new; I had had problems with that since I was a child.

However, I went to see the doctor and, after some blood tests, he said it was just the after effects of the operation and to take things easy.

Jerry and I didn't have much in the way of material things as we had both walked away from our previous relationships with nothing, so we had to start from scratch. We worked hard to gather the things we needed to make our lives a little easier for when we would eventually get our own house.

It was now coming near to the time for my agreement to end with my younger sister's house. She had decided that she was staying up north and needed to give up the house. I tried to see if Jerry and I could take over the tenancy but it was against the rules, so we had a few months to move out.

We didn't wait and immediately started looking at homes for sale and, eventually, found one and bought it.

Soon after, I went for a week to Salou, in Spain, with Jerry's sister, Rosanna. Back then, I could get holidays at a good price due to working in a travel agents and, by this time, I had moved to another shop nearer to home.

Salou was beautiful, we had a ball; going out in the nightclubs, the food and, of course, the people we met.

We had booked a day trip to Barcelona, the only trouble was we missed it and lost the money we paid too. We had been out the night before and were so drunk we couldn't get out of bed the next morning, but we had a lot of fun so it didn't bother us too much.

When we returned home, it was back to work and getting on with decorating the new house, what a mess that was. When we bought the house it wasn't in good shape but we managed to live in it.

About a week after we got back from Salou I wasn't feeling so good again, and I had missed my period, so I went along to the chemist to buy a pregnancy test kit. I had a feeling that I may have been pregnant already.

I waited until Jerry got back from work as I wanted him to be in the house when I found out so, with both excitement and anticipation, I did the test and we waited…

Oh my God! The whole street must have heard us scream with excitement when that blue line appeared, we were jumping with joy.

It must have taken us a few hours to eventually calm down, I was crying and Jerry almost certainly had tears in his eyes. I wasn't just happy about being able to have another child, I was ecstatic for Jerry because he had waited so long for this moment.

Once we had calmed down, it was time to tell the family, I wanted Jerry's mum to hear the news before anybody else; I knew how wonderful she would feel knowing her first grandchild was on its way.

When I think of all the drinking and dancing I had done in Salou, not realising I was pregnant, I was extremely lucky.

We pulled ourselves together as we planned how we were going to tell his mum. We decided we would walk into the house as normal and play it cool, then spring it on her.

Well, I have never seen someone so happy, excited and emotional as Rose, so much so that I started to cry again, so here we were both were, crying tears of joy.

Once she calmed down, Rose told us that she knew we were about to tell her I was pregnant. I asked her how she knew and she said that she could see a happy glow on both of our faces when we walked in.

Over the next few days we told the rest of the family and they were all very pleased for us.

During the next few weeks we carried on working and planning, we didn't want to start buying anything for the baby until we had had that first scan to make sure all was well.

Jerry and I decided that we wanted to go away for the New Year, so we managed to book a cheap week in Portugal. We spoke to Ben and Rachel, a couple of close friends at the time, and they said they would love to come too.

At the time, I would have preferred to go away for Christmas as that time of year had never really been my thing since all those years back when Leanne was no longer in my life. To be honest, I would have gladly dismissed Christmas all together.

This was, however, a new chapter in my life and, although I was missing Leanne and lately she was on my mind all the time, with her about to have a baby sister or brother, the idea that she would not be around for that day gave me a whole new heartache. At the same time, I knew I had to try not to let it get me down as that would not have been fair on Jerry.

Jerry and I spoke at length about the situation and he kept reassuring me that, one day, when Leanne was old enough, the truth would come out and she would see that I wasn't to blame for the fact that she ended up living with her father.

On Christmas Day we went to Rose's home for our dinner. It was a very warm and welcoming change from the last few years. Finally, I felt I actually belonged somewhere, and it was so different from all those Christmas dinners in Wales with my ex-in-laws around whom I felt I had to walk on eggshells. I guess, looking back, they thought they were something special. Perhaps, they were a little on the posh side for me but not actually 'posh' if you get my meaning.

Dinner at Rose's was lovely, with fun, laughter and just plain silliness. I loved it. Nothing was taken too seriously and the food was wonderful.

Rose was a fabulous cook, which is probably where Jerry gets it from. In fact, Jerry always said that if he hadn't gone into the construction industry he would have been a chef. The only thing that put him off, back then, was the theory part of it and I can understand why.

Some people are more practical and not everyone enjoys the academic side of things or writing. Actually, I remember when Leanne's dad and I were a couple he even used to get me to fill in all the forms, he hated it.

All the packing was done for Portugal so it was home off to bed, then up early on Boxing morning to drive to Manchester for our late afternoon flight.

We were flying from Manchester because we had been offered such an amazing deal and if we had flown from Scotland, it would have been a couple of hundred pounds more per person.

The drive down was very comfortable and we were all looking forward spending New Year (*or Hogmanay as we in Scotland call it)* in Portugal.

We got ourselves settled in the departure lounge and Jerry, Ben and Rachel went off to buy some magazines from the shop. I was just sitting there relaxing when, all of a sudden, I felt as though I was peeing myself. I quickly got up and went to the toilet.

I was in the cubicle when, all of a sudden, there was a whole lot of blood running down my leg. In total shock and horror, I let out this almighty scream and the woman in the next cubicle came running out asking if I was okay?

I explained to her that I was pregnant and she told me to stand in the corner while she went to get help. I described what Jerry, Ben and Rachel looked like and asked her to fetch them.

As I stood there in tears, I thought I had lost the baby for sure, there were all sorts running through my mind.

It seemed to be taking a long time for anyone to come to my aid so I slowly walked outside the toilets, making sure that nobody in the departure lounge could see me in that state, I stood behind a large pillar and watched for Jerry to come.

Ben arrived, as he was the first one the woman had managed to find. He was horrified to see all the blood on my trousers. Then Jerry and Rachel came. Ben went to find security to call an ambulance and, within no time at all, I was being taken through the departure lounge in a wheelchair to the ambulance.

At this point, I could see everyone's eyes upon me but, by now, I couldn't have cared less, I was more concerned for the safety our baby.

As the paramedics were helping me into the ambulance I could hear Ben say to Rachel, "I think she has lost the baby."

Well, I broke my heart and, for a moment, I felt like that scared little child again, only this time it wasn't due to domestic violence.

4
Bed Rest

I was taken to Wythenshawe Hospital in Manchester, where I was put onto a trolley bed and, to my shock, taken to this pokey little room to wait for a doctor.

Jerry stayed with me while Ben and Rachel sat in the visitors' room. I was in that little room for such a long, long time, when Ben decided enough was enough and went to reception to ask them to get me a doctor as soon as possible.

They told him that they were short staffed and would have a doctor with me as soon as they could.

Ben said, "I'm sorry, but I am watching doctors and nurses at that machine over there getting their tea and coffee. There must be someone that can see to my friend as she is pregnant and may be losing the baby."

Eventually, a nurse came in to tend me and said a doctor would be there shortly. I was lying there thinking that it was too late, as the baby must be gone by now with all that blood. Next thing, another nurse arrived and put me in a wheelchair and off I went for a scan.

That was the first scan that I had. I was around 14 weeks pregnant. The technician told me that they would have to keep me in overnight as there was a 50 per cent chance I was going to lose the baby.

I was really scared because now I knew that the baby was still there but, perhaps, I was still going to lose it.

They took me back to the room that they had put me in originally and said I had to wait for a bed.

Jerry came into the room to stay with me, then after a bit of time went off to get some tea from the machine.

While he was out of the room a nurse came in and said that I needed to move out the room as they had another emergency coming in. I assumed that I was going to a ward but, to my horror, she said that I would have to sit in the waiting room.

I totally lost my patience, "What do you mean, I need to wait in the waiting room? Are you serious? I'm lying here with nothing but a blanket to cover my bottom half and it's covered in blood and you want me to sit in a waiting room full of people? Not a chance."

She told me that they had nowhere else to put me. I was raging as she left the room.

As I was getting up to go to the waiting room Jerry walked in. "Where are you going?" he asked.

I told him what the nurse had said, and he was very angry. "Oh no you don't, lie back down and I will sort this out."

Jerry went out and spoke to the nurse. Well, actually, I think there were a few raised voices. He told the nurse that there was no way I was going to sit in the waiting room. He said that I was going to go to the visitors' room and they best sort out this situation very quickly.

Needless to say Jerry, Ben and Rachel were extremely angry and me, well, I lay down on the sofa in the visitors' room with a bloodied blanket wrapped around me. I told Jerry that there was no way I was staying in that hospital overnight. I wanted to go home and be in hospital in my hometown.

The hospital wouldn't allow me to travel home but said I could be transferred to Trafford Hospital. I would have to wait for another ambulance that end to meet the ambulance from Wythenshawe so that I could be transferred.

Four hours later they had an ambulance available and I was taken to Trafford and what a difference, not only in the way it looked, but the attention from the nurses was great.

Wythenshawe was an old wartime hospital and it was disgusting at the time I was there and for that reason I had refused to stay.

Trafford was a great hospital and they couldn't do enough for me. I had an en-suite room and they put another bed in there for Jerry to sleep on. They even had an empty room for Ben and Rachel. Not only that, they had had a leaving party for a nurse that afternoon and they brought us all food from their buffet because we hadn't eaten.

I was in Trafford for four days in total. I wasn't allowed to go home until the bleeding had stopped, and it did eventually.

The only rule was that I had to travel back to Scotland on the backseat of Jerry's work van with a pillow and blanket.

Once back in Scotland, the doctor told me that I had a low lying placenta and couldn't go back to work as I needed to have as much rest as possible. So, although I complied, I wasn't amused that I had to take time off work.

I did go back, eventually, but on the understanding that I worked part time rather than my usual full-time hours.

While I was off work I had visitors to keep an eye on me. Rose came every day and went to the shops whenever I needed anything and Jerry's dad made sure I was okay medically; one of the benefits of having someone in the nursing profession in the family.

My Aunt Ann, also a nurse, visited regularly as well and helped out where she could. I remember, one day, my aunt saying to me that an old family friend was coming to visit my parents for a few days. I was gobsmacked; I always knew that one day I would have to tell someone what he, Ron, had done to me and this was the day.

I was eight-years-old and we were living in Glasgow, he was the son of the couple who lived in the flat below us, Ron was around eighteen, maybe a little older, I'm not sure.

My parents sometimes went down to his parents' flat for a drink, and it was on these nights that Ron would come up to our flat. He used these opportunities to sexually molest me, physically and mentally.

He used to ask me to touch him, after he unzipped his trousers and brought 'it' out. I was so scared of him even now thinking about it makes me ill.

I remember another time, my mum asked me to go down to his mum's flat and borrow some sugar. His mother wasn't there but he told me to come in and he would get it. As soon as I was in he banged the door shut behind me and tried to kiss me. He started to touch me where he shouldn't have and all I could do was freeze. I was a small child and this beast would do these things; I was powerless.

Another time, his parents were in our flat having a drink with my mum and dad in the living room. I got out of bed to go to the toilet and there he was, he must have been waiting. I wanted to shout out for my mum but couldn't, I was too scared, part of me felt he may hit me and another part of me felt my mum would hit me.

Back then, and for many years after, I had many a hiding from both my parents, so I thought that if I told my mum she would give me a hiding and blame me.

You have to remember that I was a child; I didn't know any better, or what to do for the best.

That night Ron had put his penis through the letterbox and asked me to do things.

However, I said no and started to cry. He told me to shut up or my mum would hear us and I would be given a hiding. At that point I ran into the toilet.

My mum always had the windows open and, that night, the toilet window was open. Before I knew it, he had his head through the window. He said that if I didn't touch it he would shout my mum and tell her I was bad.

Every time I turned around he would be there and at every opportunity he would touch me and ask me to kiss him. I was friends with his two younger sisters and, many times, I wanted to tell them what he was doing but I was afraid they wouldn't believe me or, even worse, tell my parents and if they told them I would be in trouble.

He also had an older brother but I didn't see much of him, not that I remember anyway, he was not all there and I think he was a little backward.

I still sit and think sometimes what on earth goes through the mind of an individual who touches a child that way. Why a child? Is it that as children we are helpless?

I did everything I could to avoid ever being alone in the same room as him. Many a time I cried and, thinking back to when I was around three and a half, maybe four, I used to walk around the corner to my gran's house and there was always this heavyset man in the bushes. He used to say terrible things to scare me and here I was a scared little girl again.

We moved to a new town when I was nine and it was a huge relief never to have to see Ron again, or at least so I thought. But when I was fourteen he came to stay with my parents for a few weeks, it may have been months.

He tried it all over again, he would wait until we were alone, either in the kitchen or the living room, and he would ask me if I wanted to touch him, he would try to kiss me.

All of a sudden, I would start crying. By now he must have realised that I was older and he wouldn't be able to make me do things, but it didn't stop him from trying.

I never told my parents because I still believed I would be given a hiding.

Needless to say, sometime later, I'm not sure how long, he moved out. He moved to England somewhere. I only pray and hope that if he has children of his own that he is not doing to them and their friends what he did to me.

I told my aunt all about it, although I couldn't tell her exactly what he done to me or made me do, because it was too hurtful, not to mention disgusting. So she told my parents, because I couldn't.

Whether people want to admit it or not, when things like this happen to you, it has an impact on future relationships and there will always be something that is either said or done that will bring it all back.

5
Here We Go Again

I carried on working part time, but after about five, maybe six weeks, the bleeding started again, only this time it was just spotting, thankfully. The advice from the doctor was to stop working, so I arranged to start my maternity leave a little early.

I carried on taking things easy for the next few months until my due date. I was lying on top of my bed, one afternoon, when I thought my waters had broken, so I called the hospital to tell them that I was on my way.

They ran a few tests and assured me that I hadn't broken my waters so I went back home. They also said that the pain I was experiencing was 'Braxton Hicks'. Pretty normal, huh!

Around a week later, we had Ben and Rachel at our house for dinner, and Jerry had cooked a lovely meal. I was unusually quiet that night, as I was still having so-called 'Braxton Hicks'.

Around ten thirty that night, Rachel said it was time they were getting home. Ben looked at Jerry and said, "We aren't going anywhere. Call the hospital and tell them that Belinda will be arriving; she is going to have the baby tonight."

Jerry and Rachel looked at Ben and said together, "What?"

Ben replied, "Look at her face and her eyes. I'm telling you, she is going to have the baby."

So off we went to the hospital and, sure enough, Ben was right. They had me hooked up to a monitor the nurse told me that I had no waters. Then she left the room saying, "I'll be back in a second."

Next thing, she arrived back in the room with a couple of other nurses, a doctor and a surgeon.

Before I could ask what was going on, she said to Jerry, "We need you to sign this form, we need to operate and get the baby out as soon as possible."

I heard her say to Jerry that there was a chance that one of us may not make it.

The baby was distressed but there was something wrong with me too. I burst into tears; that scared little girl was back and with good reason. I looked at Jerry and he had gone very white, I could see the worry in his eyes.

I said to him, "If they can save the baby, then let me go."

He looked at me in horror. "What! No way," he said.

"I have a daughter already," I replied, "you have waited many years to have a child, if there is a choice to be made, then please save the baby."

He was horrified and told me to shut up and not to be so bloody stupid. He said that if we lost the baby then so be it and, if it was possible, then we would try again.

Looking back, it probably was a silly thing to say, but at the time I meant it. I wanted Jerry to have his own child, we were both thirty-three and I felt if he didn't have one then, or very soon, then he may not be able to later, and I wanted to give Rose her first grandchild.

I will never forget the look of pure pride in Jerry's face when our beautiful daughter was born. She was such a little thing only weighing six pounds, thirteen ounces. Well, I thought she was tiny because Leanne had weighed seven pounds three ounces at birth, and seemed a much bigger child.

I had had a caesarian and I was pretty much out of it the next day. I was in hospital for four days which was just as well because I was extremely sore and needed time to recover.

Jerry's sister, Rosanna, was told that same night that she was an auntie and her niece had been called Chantelle, the name Jerry picked because he heard it one night on *The Jerry Springer Show* and liked it.

We later found out that Rosanna had been in a nightclub when she heard the news and had run around screaming, "I'm an auntie." So, I think it's safe to say that she was very proud.

41

We gave Chantelle Rosanna for her middle name, after Jerry's mum, who was the proudest grandmother if ever I have seen one. Boy did she cherish her little granddaughter, as did Jerry's dad, sister and brother.

The gifts that we received from friends and family were incredible and our new baby certainly didn't run out of clothes for that first year, perhaps a little longer. Chantelle was most definitely the best dressed child around and we were so very proud or her.

I had seen Leanne, on occasion, a few months before Chantelle's birth, so she knew that I was expecting. We would kind of cross paths and say 'hi' but it was still frosty between us.

I was afraid to get too close for fear of rejection all over again, which I had had for most of my life, but it didn't have as bad an effect as the rejection from Leanne.

I think, looking back, that is probably why I was such a walkover, always trying to please and be accepted. I wanted to be loved, not just by friends but by family members too.

I don't think I'm such a pushover nowadays but I do have a way to go; I still hurt very easily, and I have issues that are unresolved and need addressing, but I'm not sure that some of them will ever be addressed.

I remember when I came home from the hospital with Chantelle, Jerry held her in his arms and said, "Our daughter will never remember me with a cigarette in my hand." He stopped that day and has never looked back. Now, that is a father's dedication to his child.

We had visitors, who arrived the day before I came home from the hospital; my dear friend, Neville, travelled up from Wales with two other friends, Phil and Graham.

They set up their tent in the garden because they felt they would be intruding with a new baby coming home with me. Fair play to them, I'm just glad it was summer! I would have felt terrible with them sleeping in a tent in the garden if it had been cold.

***

The next few months went by and we were still receiving gifts for Chantelle. Jerry and I had a caravan in Anstruther and would go away most weekends. We loved it up there by the sea, in fact, I would happily live there; it's so beautiful.

I remember one night up there while I was pregnant, around seven or eight months I think, we were in the clubhouse and here I was dancing the night away. I love music and I enjoy dancing, so I was doing the twist and Ben said to Jerry and Rachel, "Look at her dancing the twist so far gone." If there is music I'm going to dance no matter what, although I'm getting older now and the pain factor prevents me from dancing like I used to but I will still give it my best shot.

I miss our caravan and would love to have one again, but the site fees are so expensive now. There is nothing like a caravan by the sea and the sound of the seagulls first thing in the morning, or the waves coming in while you are all wrapped up on a chilly night. Yep! Those were the days.

6
Chantelle's First Birthday

Well, it was that time already and there were at Chantelle's first birthday party and I was five months pregnant. I couldn't believe it either. I always said to Jerry that everything we had gone through in life, with relationships and almost losing Chantelle, I believed God was looking down on us both, and everything that happened was and meant to be.

This pregnancy wasn't without hiccups, though, because now I was diabetic. Yep! Problems again, although nowhere near as bad as we had experienced with Chantelle.

This time I was so big I could barely move sometimes, and I suffered with constant heartburn. They told me after scans that I was expecting a huge baby, and being borderline diabetic they needed to keep an eye on me.

A few months previously, we were back and forth to the hospital with Chantelle too because we noticed that she had been dropping off to sleep at the most awkward of times and she was having muscle spasms just before falling asleep.

We noticed this for the first time when she was five months old, and they carried out some tests and tried to tell us that she had a tick, a little like a child who winks for no reason.

I didn't except that, and told the neurologist he was wrong because children didn't develop ticks until they were at least one.

I remember that it had happened to me; I used to wink at people all the time. I was one, but it only lasted a short while.

So they arranged for more tests, this time she went into the Royal Hospital for Sick Children, in Edinburgh, and was wired up around the head for 24 hours while she slept.

It was about a week later that they told us she had parasomnia disorder, a mild form of narcolepsy.

It was 12th November, 2000 and here was our other baby daughter. We called her Sinead. This time I named her and I had always loved the name Sinead. I first heard it years before when Sinead O'Connor brought out her song 'Nothing Compares To You'.

I have to say that out of my three girls, Sinead's birth was by far the most painful, so much so I wouldn't push her out at one stage. The midwife kept saying to Jerry; "Please tell Belinda she has to open her legs and push."

Of course, me being me, I said, "Piss off! I'm not doing it." (How did I think she could possibly stay in there?) We sure make a fool of ourselves under such circumstances.

Anyway, when Sinead was born the midwife took her to be washed and weighed. Then she said to me, "Belinda, you have a beautiful baby daughter weighing six pounds one ounce.

"Six pounds one ounce," I said? "Are you telling me that I went through all that bloody pain for six pounds one ounce?"

Jerry was mortified that I actually swore at the midwife but I think they have an element of forgiveness when a woman is in labour. Or at least, I hope they do!

We found out by the time Sinead was six months that she, too, was suffering from parasomnia disorder They told us that they were both the youngest children in the world to have this condition and, unfortunately, they didn't have a cure because they didn't know what causes it, other than it has something to do with a chemical in the brain that can't distinguish between sleep and being wake.

They told us that, because the girls had the condition from such a young age, they hoped that they would grow out of it by the time they were in their late teens because it normally doesn't affect people until they are in adolescence.

We were fortunate that Chantelle no longer showed signs of parasomnia disorder by the time she was around eleven, almost twelve. Sinead stopped showing signs around the age of eleven.

We were so happy because it affected both me and Jerry with lack of sleep due to the girls' night terrors and attacks through the day.

We both endured years of sleep attacks, hallucinations, night terrors and so much more with both the girls.

Jerry used to say to me, "Pack your case and go for a break to Wales," which was a godsend to me, because I was very unwell with the overactive thyroid which prevented me from getting a good night's sleep, not to mention the panics attacks etc.

I was on six Carbimazole every day. I had previously had attacks of choking and had to be hospitalised when I lived in Wales due to the condition. It wasn't until later that I discovered it could actually have killed me.

We had to take video footage of the girls having their night terrors because they were so bad and, over time, they had spasms before and after the sleep attacks.

We had to keep sharp objects away from their beds and, when they went into the sleep attack even if it was in the middle of the floor, we had to leave them there.

Many times I had been out shopping only to grab what I could, then get a taxi home. The funny thing was that they would have an attack within minutes of each other and it was no different with night terrors. Jerry and I were often exhausted.

We didn't tell everyone what we went through, only family and a few close friends because they witnessed it when it happened so we had to tell them what was wrong.

But enough about that, if I were to tell you all that happened to them, and us, through this part of their life it would be a book in itself. We had to explain to all their teachers throughout primary school about their problem, what happens and what they have to do if they had an attack. It was exhausting.

I will say, though, the video footage was a good thing because the neurologist asked us for permission to use it in their training of doctors and nurses so we said yes. I'm just glad that they no longer have the condition because if they had, then they would have had to wear medical lockets and would not have been able to use machinery or drive a car.

By the time I was expecting Sinead, Leanne and I had been in touch with one another. She was working in a footwear shop when Jerry decided to go see her and introduce himself. I'm so glad that he did because I think that was what broke the ice, although she was still a little distant.

I also think she must have been feeling really bad that we hadn't spoke for so long. I didn't blame her though; her dad and stepmother had their part to play in it, so I just went with the flow until she was ready.

It was, by now, 2001 and not only was Rosanna expecting a baby, but Leanne was too. I couldn't have been more happy about my first grandchild. I was buzzing with excitement and, now, I had to make my move as I felt maybe Leanne was too frightened to come to me. I had my reservations but I had to do it, or it could be years before we talked again, if at all.

Yes, I was very scared of being rejected but I had to do it no matter how nervous I was. I'm glad now that I reached out to her because we couldn't be more close if we tried, and here I am years later with a handsome grandson and two beautiful granddaughters, and Jerry is a wonderful grandfather.

7
Missing Rose

The date was 3rd July, 2004 and the party was in full swing for Chantelle's fifth birthday. We had hired the local sports centre for her party with a disco and bouncy castle and, of course, Jerry had prepared the food.

It was another great day and lots of Chantelle's little friends had come to the party. They were all having a ball and the adults were also having a rare time too.

Rose wasn't looking too well and I'd not seen her look unwell like that before. She always had such a happy glow but on that day she really didn't look herself.

We were all enjoying the party and Rose did too, but I could see it was a struggle for her. Chantelle had a great time, as did Sinead; they love a good party.

A couple of weeks later, Rose took a turn for the worse and had to go into hospital. She wasn't well at all and didn't look good.

She was only supposed to be in hospital over the weekend and we went to see her on the Saturday afternoon, on 17th July. Rose looked much better, almost back to herself again, and they said she would be going home the next day. Rosanna had gone to see her with her daughter in the evening.

I will never forget the phone call we received that night. We were watching the lottery results when the phone rang. It was Jerry's dad.

"Belinda, is Jerry there?" he asked gravely. I knew by the tone of his voice that something was very wrong. I handed the phone to Jerry and, a second later, he started shouting, "No, not my mum," over and over again. He was breaking his heart.

I didn't know what to do and, by this time, I was sobbing too. Jerry was running around crying, trying to find his jacket, even though he knew were the jacket was, he was in such a state he couldn't think straight. He just kept repeating, "Not my mum."

Jerry drove to the hospital to be with his dad, Rosanna, and his brother, John. I stayed at home and called my parents to tell them the sad news that Rose had passed away. They said that they would be with me in ten minutes. My aunt was working in the hospital that night and I also called to tell her. She went to the ward to be with Jerry and the rest of the family.

Then I called Jerry's best friend, down south, then Ben and Rachel. Everyone was absolutely gutted as Rose was such a well-liked woman. Everyone loved her and those closest to her were completely heartbroken. It destroyed Jerry.

Rose should have been coming out of hospital the following day and, when we saw her, she looked great so we couldn't get our head round why this had happened.

It turned out that she had suffered an aneurism. Rose was never one to have people run after her and, when Rosanna had left on the Saturday night, Rose had got out of bed to ask for her medication rather than ring for the nurse. She got to the door and collapsed.

The aneurism went straight to her heart. That was it; she was gone. We were told that she didn't suffer and, although we know this and are glad that she didn't, Jerry, John and Rosanna have suffered ever since.

Chantelle and Sinead remember a lot about Rose considering they were only four and five when she passed away. They often talk about the things she did that made them happy, which ends in tears, but I don't stop them from crying as I believe it lifts a huge amount of stress from them. Holding it in would only cause their heart to break even more.

We visit Rose's grave often and the girls do too. We miss her so much and it hurts that she was so young, only 58, when she died. It makes me sad when I think of Rose's own heartbreak through the years. She lost her brother, Frances, just a few months before she passed away.

Rose lost both of her parents within months of each other, back in 1978, and she never really got over it. Then she lost her brother, Michael, in 1996, he was only in is forties and she took losing him very hard indeed.

Michael and Rose were very close, and Jerry looked on him like a father figure as he never knew his real dad. His stepdad only came into his life when he was around twelve, so for all of those years he was pretty much on his own until his sister and brother came along.

We gave Sinead, Michaela for her middle name after Michael, who has a daughter Michaela. Michaela often jokes with us and says we should have called her Michaela Sinead, instead of Sinead Michaela. I sometimes wish that we had of done that too.

The weeks after the funeral were pretty much a blur. There were a lot of people at the funeral because Rose was such a well-loved lady.

Her nephew played the bagpipes at the funeral and I have to say he moved us to tears. We were all sitting in the garden that morning while he was practicing and, when he hit the notes from 'Amazing Grace', that really set everyone off. There must have been around twelve of us crying our eyes out. It was a beautiful service, but extremely sad and the whole day exhausted us.

Chantelle and Sinead didn't come to the funeral for obvious reasons; they were much too young. They were completely devastated at the loss of Rose, even at that age, and more so Chantelle who kept looking up at the stars for her gran.

Rose will be looking down on us all with pride, proud of her children and her grandchildren. Rosanna has a little girl, Nicole, who was one when Rose passed away, and she was also expecting her second child, Kieran. I can't begin to imagine how she must have felt when her mum passed away without meeting her first grandson.

His name is engraved with his sister's, along with Chantelle and Sinead, on her gravestone so, for us, that is a comfort. I know Rose is looking down on us all and I often sense her around the house too.

8
Operation Time Again

Well, there I was again; tired, lethargic and having more panic attacks. Blood tests revealed that my thyroid was giving cause for concern. I started to get burry vision and headaches, so I went to the optician thinking I needed to change my glasses.

The optician said that I needed to see my doctor but didn't say why. I made the appointment a few days later and when I saw the doctor he told me that I had Graves disease and needed to have the operation and not the radioactive iodine treatment that was originally planned.

He said that if they didn't operate quickly I would end up with bulging eyes, and more serious problems.

"Bulging eyes," I said, "You had better get that operation in place as soon as possible, because if I end up with bulging eyes I will never set foot outside my house again."

I only waited a few months for the operation, but those months were horrible. I had a feeling inside my gut that said to me, *I should not be going in for this operation.*

For some reason I knew, or felt, that I would not come out of that hospital again, not because Rose went in and didn't come out, which is what Chantelle believed. She associated hospitals with death. The poor girl refused to go into hospital because she thought that anyone who went into hospital died. It took us a couple of years to make her understand that wasn't the case.

I felt I wouldn't come through the operation, I mean, I really felt it right up until the day of the operation.

I was given a pill to make me sleepy ready for when I went to theatre. Jerry sat with me until it was time, when the porter eventually came to say they were ready to take me down.

Jerry gave me a kiss and said, "I will see you tonight."

Then he left, and the next thing I knew a nurse came and said to me, "I'm sorry, Belinda, but we are unable to take you for your operation."

I said, "What do you mean?" Then the surgeon came in and explained that the sterilised equipment they needed hadn't arrived from the Royal Infirmary in Edinburgh. In a way, I was glad because I still felt I was not coming out of that hospital had they continued with the op.

The weird thing is, Jerry later told me that after he left me he went into the hospital chapel to say a prayer for me. So I think, to this day, that the operation was meant to be canceled. Maybe it sounds a little crazy to some people, but to me it's what I believe.

I didn't have to wait long before they rescheduled the operation, less than two months, and I no longer had those awful feelings so, yes, I still think it wasn't meant to be the first time. They removed seven eighths of the thyroid so I still had a little left in, which they said I may have to have removed later on in life. So now I had an under-active thyroid and would be on medication for the rest of my life. Oh the joys!

I think that's why Jerry and I are so well-matched; we have an unbelievable amount in common. He also has an under-active thyroid, so our girls are sure to have this problem also, later in life.

Jerry and I often laugh when we talk about the traits we share; sometimes we say the same thing at the same time, or we are thinking exactly the same thing, it's so uncanny.

Neither of us have met our biological fathers and both our mothers were conductors on the buses back in Glasgow.

We both enjoy mostly the same things and we have a very close, loving bond, not only with each other but with our children and grandchildren.

Jerry is not only a wonderful father and grandfather, he is also a wonderful husband, my best friend and, most definitely, my soul mate. I don't know where I would be without him.

Rose and my mum got on very well too, they were both of the old school so you can imagine the topics of conversation between them. Rose was only a couple of years younger than my mum and I know that Mum thought a lot of Rose.

Jerry and I used to laugh when we had them both round to the house. My dad and Jerry's dad would sit talking away in the living room while both our mums would be in the kitchen with a glass of beer and a cigarette, chatting about their days back in Glasgow and who knows what else.

I've always been very emotional and sensitive and would cry at the slightest thing, especially when it comes to others.

I like to be there for people in their time of need. I'm especially good in a crisis, except when it comes to myself, then my natural instincts go haywire which has often led to me making bad decisions in the past, and even now sometimes.

It doesn't matter how rough I've had it in the past, I've always been very optimistic. I'm in love with the idea that good things will come.

I have an easygoing nature too, probably too easygoing, I have the need to express myself and will do anything for peace and harmony.

I've never liked to hear raised voices and will do anything to avoid such situations; that's one of the things Jerry found quite disturbing about me. One time he raised his voice, not in an argument, it was something he was telling me that happened and he raised his hand and I flinched.

Jerry told me, sometime later, that he was a little upset when he saw me flinch and take a step back. I wasn't even aware that I had done it.

Because he mentioned it, I did, on occasion, recognise the fact that this was something I did. Maybe it was a reaction caused by everything that happened over the years, I don't think I do it now, or certainly not that I've noticed.

One of my biggest faults is indecision, which has resulted in me missing many good opportunities. I have a placid, patient and reasonably forgiving nature, but do me a wrong, or those I love, and I can be very forceful in my actions. I'm not talking about a fist fight here. I can do so much damage with that mouth of mine and I definitely wouldn't want to be on the other side of it.

It was a shame, though, that I didn't use it back when I was being battered and abused, but I was young and naive, not like the woman I am today. If I'm being honest, I can still be a little naive, but not as stupid.

The things that I have experienced in life have made me appear cynical at times, but my independent and down to earth attitude conceals a sentimental heart and a disposition that is, essentially, friendly.

One of my regrets is that I didn't put my strong business instincts to better use but, you never know, there is still time and who knows what the future holds.

One thing is for sure, there were many personal complications and much disillusion in the first thirty years of my life.

9
Secrets and Lies

I was pregnant with Chantelle when I received the phone call, at two-thirty in the morning. Jerry answered the phone, then woke me, and said it's your uncle for you.

"Listen, Belinda," my uncle told me, "your dad is not your real dad."

Still befuddled by sleep, I said, "Say that again," going into the hall so as not to keep Jerry awake.

My uncle repeated, "Your dad is not your dad, I've spoken to your mother and told her that she needs to tell you the truth."

I had suspected for many years that something was being kept from me and, on occasion, I did try to question my uncle when he had had one too many to drink. What is it they say? 'A drunk man always tell the truth'. So I used those opportunities to ask the dreaded question.

He would never tell me though. He would say, "Belinda, if I was to tell you anything I would cause a lot of trouble. If you want to know anything, ask your mum."

Of course, I never did. I was too afraid she would smack me one; I was always afraid of my parents so I never dared to upset them or, at least, I tried not to.

I asked my aunt once if there was something being kept from me and she said she didn't know what I was talking about. I've always known when my uncle and aunt were lying, and I knew then too.

I left it but, on and off, I would bring the subject up and, again, they would tell me nothing.

Now, though, I had my answer. I knew my uncle had been drinking, I could tell by the sound of his voice, but I was glad that he had finally told me.

I couldn't face my mum the next day, I was in shock, even though I knew deep down that one of them wasn't my parent.

Instead, I called my aunt but she was out, so I spoke to my cousin who had also been told by my uncle that my dad wasn't my real dad. Needless to say, it didn't go down well with my parents that he had told my cousin, let alone me.

It was two days after I had received the news that I plucked up the courage to visit my mum. I remember my stomach being in knots with worry, at the same time thinking to myself: *Why the hell should I be the one feeling like this?* The truth of the matter was that I was still afraid of my parents, when you have had as many hidings as I've had over the years, it makes you feel you are nothing and leaves you with a sense of fear.

I walked into the living room my mum was sat on the chair. I asked where my dad was she said that he was in the kitchen, but he wouldn't come through to face me. She said that he was worried I wouldn't want to know him anymore.

I told her that, as far as I was concerned, he was the only father I've ever known and it didn't make any difference to me.

In truth, I was too afraid to tell her that I was hurting and that what they had done, keeping this secret for all those years, made me angry and tore me in two.

I was also afraid that she would cry and be upset if I told them both what I really thought of them; there I go again thinking of others' feelings before my own.

Don't get me wrong, a part of me did feel sorry for my dad, he must have been feeling awful, but how did they think I felt on hearing this.

They had had so many opportunities to come clean such as when I turned sixteen, or after I came out of hospital in Wales, knowing that I could have died, or when I was asked by the doctor if there was any family history with thyroid or throat problems.

I asked my mum years later, "Why didn't you come to Wales to the hospital when I called to say how sick I was?" (I was hooked up to a drip because I had pleurisy and pneumonia.)

"We didn't have the money to get there," she replied. I have to say that if my daughter had been lying in a hospital bed, not sure if she was going to make it, I would have borrowed money if necessary and would have been on the first train down there.

It all fell into place when I went to ask about my biological father. I got no answers, well none that I needed to know.

My mum said that my real father had walked away when she told him she was pregnant. The trouble is, I've heard tree different versions of that story so now I don't believe any of them.

I decided that I would leave things alone because I was getting nowhere, although I did find out his name was Thomas. At one point, I wondered if I should look for him but thought better of it.

The strange thing is that, over a seventeen-year period, I had been to several mediums and they always said to me, "I have your father here." I could never understand why they said that because, prior to me finding out the truth, I told them that my father was very much alive, but they would say, "No, this man is telling me he is your dad."

They also told me his name was Tom or Tam and that I looked like him, right down to the curly hair.

One medium even told me that, for the first half of my life, I was doomed to live a humdrum, uneventful existence rather to experience life to the full. Well, that was most certainly true but I wasn't about to settle for second, best nor did I!

There is no doubt that in my character there is a lot of quiet strength, moral courage and persistence. I do actually have a backbone when I need it. Push my button too many times and I lose it big time so, over the coming months, I was a ticking time bomb. The only thing that stopped me losing control was the thought of hurting others.

A couple of years later, when I was visiting my uncle, I said to him that I was going to go through to Bridgeton, Glasgow, to where my father grew up. I had found out where he had lived when he dated my mum and I figured if I visited a couple of pubs in the area, there were bound to be older men in there who knew my dad.

I decided to look for him, initially, for medical reasons. I had so many issues that I needed to know if they came from that side of the family as it didn't come from my mum's side.

Deep down, though, I was curious. I wanted to see what he looked like, but also wanted to hear his side of the story.

Yes, very often I will sit on the fence, but then I get nosy and I need the truth, no matter how much it may hurt, and I knew I wasn't going to get it from my mum.

My uncle told me a story about my dad well, a couple of stories, and said to me that if I went looking for him and he found out that someone had been asking questions about him, it could cause a lot of trouble or I could get hurt. I won't go into the reasons why! I thought it best to take his advice and leave well alone, I didn't want anything happening to my family.

My uncle did tell me what my dad looked like and said I looked very much like him. He said that was where I got my clean, well-dressed style from, and my manners.

That made me feel good. I was never an untidy person, my home was always clean and tidy and so was I.

I would never go out of the house without looking my best and, back in the day, I had my share of admirers, if not more than most.

My father was a bit of a looker, apparently, and had plenty of women falling at his feet; he too was a well-dressed man who took care of himself. He always wore a suit and tie, according to my uncle, and this was confirmed to me years later.

10
Family Tree

It's amazing what falls out of the closet when researching your family tree, and mine is no exception.

A few years after being told about my biological dad I decided to start looking for him. My health was continuing to give cause for concern and the doctor asked me to try and find out if there were certain health issues on my dad's side of the family.

It took me a few years to gather information about my dad due to the fact that my mum refused to talk about him and I was always too scared to sit her down and tell her that I wanted answers. However, I did have enough to go on to visit the registry office and see what I could dig up.

I had been researching our family tree, on and off, for a few years on my mother's side and I also started looking into Jerry's side of the family which took me way back to Ireland.

My mother's family came from Antrim in Ireland, some moved later to Campbeltown, in Scotland, and were farmers.

Some of the stories I remember as a child would make your hair curl; about my great grandmother, for example, who, by all accounts, was a bit of gangster – well that's the word I would use!

She was a money lender and, apparently, those who didn't pay up had to pay the price and she would send her henchmen round to kneecap them. I have to say that, as a youngster, I found this all to be quite fascinating. I loved anything to do with the Mafia etc but, obviously, when I grew up I soon realised that it wasn't something to brag about.

Looking at photos of her I could see that she wasn't someone to be messed with and, back then, a lot of woman had to be hard, although perhaps not quite as forceful as she was.

If I could have one wish, though, it would be that my mother's parents were still alive when I was born.

Sadly my grandmother passed away aged just forty-two, when my mum was fifteen and my granddad two, years before I was born.

I went to the Registry Office in Edinburgh to ask for their help in finding more information about my dad and I gave the female clerk the only details I had: *Thomas McGinty, living in Bridgeton Glasgow around 1964 onwards.* I told her that he was around five years older than my mum and that he would have been born around 1937.

I sat there in anticipation while she typed the details into her computer, then she said, "I've found him."

My stomach was doing summersaults with excitement. Then, to my horror, she said to me, "I'm very sorry but it looks like he passed away."

The smile on my face turned to sadness and I think she could see it. The clerk continued: "His name is Thomas McGinty, born in 1935, he passed away in 1992 aged fifty-six." I was devastated and asked her if she was sure it was my dad. She replied, "Yes, there was only one Thomas McGinty living in Bridgeton and he has definitely passed away." She also told me that he had been born in Bridgeton too.

I asked her what he died of and she said she couldn't tell me, but I could order a copy of his death certificate which would fill in the blanks.

I ordered it right there and then, I also ordered a copy of his birth certificate. It took all of my strength not to cry, and I felt extremely sick.

At that point, I can't tell you the hatred I felt for certain people. I've never hated anyone but, right then, I did and I couldn't shake off that feeling for the rest of the day.

I took the certificates home and sat there for what seemed like hours just looking at them, it gave his address at the time of death, his occupation and his date of birth, he was born in the same month as me.

As I looked further down and read that the cause of death was 'pulmonary oedema, acute myocardial infection and ischaemic heart disease'. I ran to the toilet and was violently sick. I was shaking and my heart had that very sad, empty feeling.

I felt sad that my dad had passed away at such a young age, but at the same time very angry that I hadn't been told about him sooner.

I was only twenty-seven when he died, and if I hadn't had the right to know him taken from me, I would have had time with him. I should have been told.

I will never be able to forgive my parents for not telling me about my dad. What right did they have to take away my choice to know him or have him in my life?

So, now I was on a mission to find out if I had grandparents that were still living. At one point I thought, *That's it, it's over I can't move forward*, but I so wanted to.

I needed closure and the more I thought about my dad, the more I wanted to know, and I still needed to know about health conditions.

I went back to the Registry Office. I had never seen so many records in one place. I loved going there; it was so peaceful and tranquil, definitely a place to have quiet time and gather your thoughts.

Using my dad's birth and death certificates I put the relevant information into the computer and waded my way through hundreds of records.

I will say to anyone wanting to trace their family tree 'be prepared'; it's time consuming and can be very frustrating at times but, with patience and hard work, you will get there. I would love to do this for other people, I'm totally hooked.

Bit by bit, I started to uncover my dad's family starting with his parents. My granddad's name was James McGinty and he had also passed away but I noticed on his death certificate it said 'For the Procurator Fiscal'. I wondered what had happened there then.

His death certificate stated that he had died of burns injuries, so I had to look for the court papers to find out how and why.

My grandfather was born in 1908, and I'm not sure if he was in the Army or the Navy, but I know he served his time. Apparently, it was a house fire that resulted in his death, in 1966, when he was only fifty-eight.

I have a fear of fire because, when I was in my teens, my mum had a fire caused by a chip pan, hence why I would never have one.

My grandmother was called Thomasina and her father was in the military but was killed in action.

Her mother was called Belinda Conniss and both sides of my dad's family originated from Ireland too. That Irish blood runs through my veins for sure and I'm very proud of my heritage.

I've managed to go as far back as 1836 on my dad's side of the family but still have a way to go. Unfortunately, because of the war in Ireland, and the burning of important records which, I have to add, was a mistake, because the Irish thought they were burning our records when in fact it was their own.

I have another trip to Ireland planned to gather the rest of the records that I can't get in Scotland, so I'm looking forward to that.

11
Extended Family

So there I was, a few years later, with a whole new family. I started to add some names to Facebook in the hope that I could find my dad's family and I joined groups from Glasgow.

It was some months before I started to get feedback from people, who either knew the area my dad came from or knew the family. Then, one day, I received a private mail from a man who said he knew one of the names I was looking for.

He told me that he lived across the street from this man, so I asked him to enquire if he might be the person I was looking for.

The name I gave him was that of my dad's brother. I knew his name because it was on my dad's death certificate, as he was the person who signed for it.

A couple of days later, he got back to me and said that the man who lived opposite him was the son of my uncle, my uncle had passed away too.

We eventually set up a meeting and I went to Glasgow, full of nerves, although there was no need because it actually turned out really well, and he was a very nice man.

His name was Robert and I was welcomed into his home. We spoke to each other as if we had known each other for years. His wife was also there. Robert told me that as I was walking across the road to towards him he could see right away I was the image of my dad.

I asked him if he had any photos of my dad but, unfortunately, he didn't. Robert did, however, have photos of my uncle and one with him and his sister with my uncle. There was also a group photo of my granddad with his Army buddies.

Robert told me that, years previously, he remembers my dad in the kitchen with his mum, saying to her, "I have a daughter out there and I need to find her." That was his only recollection of the conversation. He could remember nothing else other than my dad knew that I existed.

Robert said that there was a photo of my dad, but he believed one of his sisters, Agnes, had it and that, in the photo, my dad was sitting with his Alsatian dog. So I set up a meeting with her.

Agnes was pleasant enough but I could see that she was a little nervous about meeting me, which was understandable, after all, she didn't know me at all.

Agnes gave me a little of the family history but, again, no photo. I did find it a little strange that nobody seemed to have a photo of my dad, or was it that they just didn't want me to have one?

I did say to all of them that I would copy any photos with my iPad as I didn't like to take anything away. They were their memories.

Agnes told me about another daughter of my uncle, who lived down south, and said that I should get in touch with her.

I did contact her but, unfortunately, she didn't know anything about my dad because her mum moved down south when she was a baby.

Eventually, I went back to the Registry Office, now that I had gathered more information and names. It was through the information I had that I found my dad's wives, when he married them, and where they lived.

Only one child came up with his first wife and that was my brother, Thomas. I managed to find my brother's marriage certificate and, through that, I found an old address.

I was amazed when I found that the address was only a couple of miles from where I lived, so I arranged to go to the house.

The couple who lived there at the time told me that the people I was looking for no longer lived there but she did give me the name and address of a woman who had known the family for many years.

By this time I was buzzing with excitement. I went to the lady's house shaking a little, because I was getting closer to finding the answers to my questions.

The lady invited me into the house after I had told her who I was and why I had come to see her. She was a lovely lady and told me more than my dad's family had been able to.

A little of what she told me was that she had been friends with the family for many years and knew my brother and his wife, and also knew my dad. She said that my brother's daughter still lived in the area but her mum had passed away. She said that Thomas lived in Glasgow.

Then she gave me the address of my niece, Pauline, and her telephone number and said that I should go to her house and talk to her. I didn't as I wanted to phone her first to explain who I was rather than just turning up on the doorstep.

I went home feeling both tired from such a long day but very excited because I had found a niece who lived in the same area.

I was, however, a little apprehensive about calling Pauline straight away. What if she didn't want to know or what if she just hung up the phone? If she had done that, then that would have been the end of my search, because I wouldn't have been able to take the rejection.

I waited until my girls were in bed before calling because if there was a problem, I didn't want them to see me cry.

I started to dial the number then got scared, so hung up. It took me three attempts to do so but the third time it rang out. Part of me was relieved, I just didn't know how to start the conversation.

Around an hour later, my phone rang, it was my niece. I picked up the phone and the voice said, "Hello! I had a missed call from you." My first thought was: *She has a strong Glaswegian accent.*

"Hi!" I said, "I'm not sure how to tell you this but I think I might be your aunt..." There was a pause and I asked her if her dad was called Thomas McGinty?

"Yes," she replied.

I said, "Well, I'm his sister."

I went on to ask her who her granddad was and she confirmed the name, so I told her the story.

Pauline was pleasantly surprised and very nice to talk to. I was glad that she had taken the news so well and very happy when she told me she would call her dad and tell him about me.

I asked Pauline to give him my phone number, as I would like to speak to him once he had had time to take it all in. Pauline promised that she would call me after she had spoken to him.

78

Pauline called me the next day and I asked her how her dad had taken the news?

Apparently, she had said to him, "Dad, I received a call from a woman who says that she is your sister."

Thomas replied, "WHAT?" My niece had repeated it again and her dad had asked her who I was, my name etc.

Pauline said that she had given him my phone number but that he needed time to process what he had just been told.

I told her that was fine as it was a lot to take in. Then I asked her if she had any photos of my dad as, up to that point, nobody seems to have one. My niece said that she did have a photo but would need time to dig it out as it was with her mum's things. All of her mum's belongings had been put away as she had passed away the previous year.

I said that was fine, I would wait, and I was sorry to hear about her mum.

We arranged to get together and go for a cup of tea so that she could meet me. So, I picked her up a week later and off we went. As soon as she got in the car she said to me, Belinda, you look so like my dad.

I smiled and said, "Really?" Pauline said she would arrange for photos of her dad too. I asked her if I would be able to go and meet him and she replied that he did want to meet me, but not yet, which was fair enough.

We chatted about all sorts of things, including the family history, of course. Pauline told me a lot about my dad and I was so happy that, finally, I was learning about my roots and my family history was all coming together.

It turned out that Pauline worked in the local chip shop, which I had been to on several occasions not even knowing that she was my niece.

Pauline has three children, and a brother who also has three children, so not only was I an aunt again, but I was a great aunt too. Now, I really was starting to feel my age!

12
The Moment I Had Been Waiting For

I had spoken to my niece on several occasions when, one night, I noticed that I had private mail on Facebook. Pauline had sent several photos of herself and her brother, their children and my brother when he was younger.

Oh my God! When I saw my brother I couldn't believe how much we did look alike and our Sinead looked like him too.

Then, in another message, was a photo of my dad with his dog. I was shaking as, right away, I printed a copy and sat there looking at the image for some time.

Jerry was working in Jerusalem at the time so I emailed him a copy of the photos. I then went upstairs to the girls to show them the pictures. I said to Chantelle, "I have a photo of my dad."

"Let me have a look," she replied. Then I broke down in a flood of tears and she said to me "Oh Mum, I'm so happy for you."

I was on a high for days afterwards and couldn't stop looking at his photo.

When I spoke to Jerry the next day he could tell how happy I was. My perseverance had paid off and he was pleased that I now had closure.

Jerry and I spoke via video message as he works overseas for the United Nations. He comes home every seven weeks, for a week, which is great because we are actually able to spend so much time together as a family. When he worked in the UK it was early starts and late finishes most of the time so he really only got to see the girls for an hour before school and for an hour or so in the evening.

When he was home we were together more or less round the clock, which meant we could all do so much more and see each other all the time.

Jerry always wanted to work overseas, although it did take him a week to persuade me to let him go. I'm glad that I did now as he has been awarded a gold medal, not to mention having had several promotions, for his hard work. I'm so proud of him.

By now I had a dozen or so photos of nieces, nephews and my brother, but only one of my dad. However, that was okay by me; one was better than none.

When I decided to research the rest of the family tree I wanted to continue with my dad's side because, even though he had passed away, I felt I needed to know more about him and his family, such as grandparents etc.

I had a call from my niece to say that my brother would like to meet me, so we arranged to get the train to Glasgow a couple of weeks later.

That couple of weeks seemed like months and the closer it got the more nervous I was, not because I was going to meet him, but because I was worried that once we met me he may not want to see me again, let alone be a part of my life.

I couldn't have been more wrong, as soon as we walked into his home he gave me and the girls a kiss and hug, which really broke the ice.

So there we were myself, Chantelle, Sinead, my niece and nephew, Thomas and his wife. I felt so comfortable with them because we were given such a warm welcome.

Thomas and I do look alike and have similar traits. He told me about our dad and also said that we have two other brothers who are younger than him (Thomas is the oldest of us all). Thomas was in touch with them briefly and saw them at our dad's funeral but lost contact with them after that. He also told me that he knew about me and that years ago our dad said he had a sister, but the subject was never brought up again.

So, not only do I have three sisters and a brother by my stepdad, but three older brothers with my dad.

I was happy; when I was growing up I hated being the oldest and always wished I had an older sister or brother, now I had three.

I used to tell people that my aunt was my older sister and my uncle was my older brother, in reality I was just a lonely little soul.

I wondered for a time if I should try to contact my other brothers. Thomas and I discussed them briefly, after which I decided I wouldn't look for them.

Besides, I had Thomas, assuming he wanted to be involved with us and, I'm happy to say, he does, for which I am eternally grateful.

Another funny thing is that, when I was younger, I always said that if I ever had a son I would call him Thomas, because I've always liked the name – a little spooky looking back now.

I know that one of my other brothers is called Paul but I'm not sure the name of the other one. My dad was married three times, he had Thomas with his first wife but no children with the other two, well not that I'm aware of, so I can only assume that Paul and my other brother are by another relationship.

My dad appeared to have had his fair share of women in his life, but then he was a looker. I'm just sorry I never got the chance to meet him.

He had long, curly, fair hair and I have been told that he was always immaculately dressed and was a gentleman. I remember being in the Barras in Glasgow (a large open market) and speaking to a woman called Anna, a lovely lady, who, it turned out, had been a friend of my dad since the age of twenty-one. Anna told me that I looked very much like him.

I asked her if she might have an old photo of Dad when he was younger, but she said no. Back then, she explained, they didn't have many photos taken and some avoided having their photo taken for various reasons. I understood what she was talking about!

I showed her a photo of my brother when he was younger and, as soon as she looked at it, she said "Well, you don't need to have a photo of your dad when he was young, because he looked exactly like your brother." So that was the best I got. Now, I just look at Thomas's photo of when he was younger and I see my dad.

Through time, I spoke to a distant cousin of my dad's, called Brian, and he was able to fill me in on a lot of things that nobody else could, or would, including everything I had already been told.

Brian told me that I had another brother that neither I nor Thomas knew about and said that he would have been forty-two then. So he would be about forty-five now. Another brother to add to the list, I wonder if there are more? My dad did tell him about me, and Brian said my dad had tried to find me years ago.

He said that my dad was a very private man and didn't go around telling everyone about his children, nor did he want people to know his business.

My dad knew how to handle himself too, apparently, and it would have been a very brave man who wanted to cause problems. My dad would have dealt with the matter quietly.

Brian told me that my dad worked hard and often would travel backwards and forwards to England. I know that my dad also spent some time in Australia but nobody seems to know why, so I guess he was, indeed, a very private man.

13
Treasured Possessions

Rolling forward a couple of years and I now have much more information about my dad. My niece knew that I didn't have anything that belonged to him so she gave me a couple of things that I hold close to my heart.

One of these items is a watch that he wore. He had quite a few so I was glad she still had some to keep. I keep it in a very safe place and, every once in a while, I take it out and just hold it.

She also gave me one of his 'sashes'; my dad was an Orangeman and, for those who are not familiar with the term, he was a member of the Protestant Orange Lodge.

I wasn't surprised by this news, as my mum was a member of the Lodge when she was younger, not something that I agree with, only because of the trouble it has caused over the years. I have to say that, if it was up to me, I would ban it altogether and the Catholic one too.

I remember, as a child, being made to walk in the marches but, as soon as my mum was out of view, I would run and hide; I hated it.

I have another photo of my dad now, that Thomas gave me, and a couple of photos of my grandmother. I was told that I looked like her too and, yes, there is definitely a resemblance.

Unfortunately, my dad was cremated and I was really sad when I learnt that he hadn't been buried because it meant that I wasn't able to visit his grave.

So, I registered and signed a special tribute to my dad at the crematorium where he was cremated, and soon I am having a plaque made to be laid there in his memory.

Although I only have the two photos of my dad I will treasure them always. Last year, I organised a 50th birthday party for Jerry and was so happy that Thomas, my niece, her fiancé and daughter, my nephew and his wife came. Unfortunately, my sister-in-law had to work.

It was a great night. Thomas and the rest of the family really enjoyed themselves and I felt very special because there I was, dancing with my big brother, and I felt so proud. I was quite upset that my parents didn't come to the party, but then I had a feeling they wouldn't because I had warned them beforehand that my brother and his family would be there.

I was a little upset that they would miss their son-in-law's 50th birthday because of Thomas, but then I thought, *I'm not going to feel guilty* and there was no way I wouldn't invite my brother.

It wasn't mine or Thomas's fault that my mum and dad didn't stay together.

Thomas told his mum about me and I was happy to hear that she held no malice towards me. Thomas didn't have any other siblings other than our other brothers.

I was told by family members that my dad had his knuckles tattooed on both hands one with the name 'Dave' and the other with the name 'Pete'. I later found out that his brother (my Uncle James) had the same tattoos. To this day, I still don't know who Dave and Pete are and neither do the rest of the family.

I often wonder if perhaps they had two other brothers; twins maybe? I had had twins! Unfortunately, I didn't know this until I visited a medium. It sounds crazy, I know, but this is how it all unfolded.

The medium told me that I had a little girl by my side and that she is always around me. He asked me if I had ever lost a child. I said no, not that I was aware of. I then told him there was reason to believe, years ago, that I may have been pregnant when they sterilised me and, maybe, that's where this came from. I had been told about this little girl by several mediums over the years.

I told him, "I'm not aware of having had a miscarriage and I've never had an abortion because I'm against it."

He then went on to tell me that it was an incident that happened whereby I lost so much blood they thought I was going to lose the child. Then he added, "She is the twin of your daughter now."

I was, by this time, shaking because I realised he was talking about the time I was rushed to Wythenshawe Hospital when I was expecting Chantelle.

After the reading, which I had recorded and still have, I decided to check this out. I have visited several mediums over the years and I still don't know if they can really get messages from the other side. Unless they can tell me something only I know, then I think they are a waste of time and money.

I told Jerry about the reading and, although I could see he was feeling a little upset, he told me I should get proof before I let this upset me.

I didn't tell anyone, not even the doctor, because I didn't want to give him the chance to destroy any of my medical notes. I called the doctor's receptionist and asked her to give me a copy of my medical notes from 1991 until 2014.

She said it would cost me £13 and I said that was fine, then all I had to do was wait a couple of days to receive my notes.

A couple of days later, I had a call from the doctor's surgery to say that my notes were ready to pick up. With a little apprehension I drove down to pick them up, paid the money and returned home.

There were quite a lot of notes as they dated back to the year I married for the first time and, as I have a few medical conditions, there was bound to be plenty of reading in there.

I sat down with my cup of tea and started to read through everything. Then I got to December 1998. Low and behold, there it was in black and white, totally confirming what the medium had said, I had indeed lost a child; 'Chantelle's twin'. I broke my heart and writing this now, I'm sat here full of emotion for my little girl.

It turned out that I had miscarried her when I started bleeding at the airport. I was totally shocked like you wouldn't believe, and I was shaking and crying.

I called Jerry to tell him that, yes, we had lost a child. He was livid, but emotional too.

Jerry said that I should make an appointment for the next time he was home for us to talk to the doctor together. We wanted answers.

I asked the doctor why? Why hadn't they told me that I had lost a child? He said that, because of the stress I was already under at the time of the bleeding, I may have lost Chantelle too, and that's why the doctor wouldn't have told me.

I asked him why they hadn't told me after I gave birth to Chantelle, but he couldn't answer that question.

I was advised to sue the NHS for failing to tell us, but it had gone way past the three year deadline so we couldn't.

As yet, we still haven't told Chantelle and Sinead about their sister, one reason being that it has taken us quite some time to get our heads around the fact and we were both still grieving. Secondly, Chantelle has been sitting exams for the past couple of years, and is now taking her Highers (exams in Scotland, equivalent to A-levels) and we don't want to put any stress on her until she has finished school.

14
The Pain

Pain! It's such a small word yet can cause the biggest heartbreak. For days, weeks and months I couldn't stop thinking about Rosie. That's what I named her.

The medium told me, that same day, that my little girl was always around me. He said that she has had a snoop around my room, she loved my jewellery and that I had some really nice clothes, but insisted I stop wearing black so much.

That's quite funny really because I was nicknamed the 'Black Widow' by some of my friends because they only ever saw me in black, so that made me chuckle.

She also said that she liked my tattoo. I have 'Jerry' tattooed at the bottom of my back. *How could he know these things*? I thought to myself.

I went to see that same medium the year after I confirmed all that he had told me and, in my reading, he told me that my little girl said thank you for giving her a name. I broke down in a flood of tears because, yes, I had given her a name but I haven't told anyone other than Jerry.

Why did I name her Rosie? When our Chantelle was a toddler, and until she left primary school, she would call her teddy 'Rosie'. She used to say that if she had a dog she would name her Rosie too.

How strange is that? I remember only around six years ago Chantelle had started screaming in her room. She called out to us and Jerry ran up the stairs, I didn't go but, instead, stood by the back door.

For some reason I knew that she had seen something. Anyway, she was crying her eyes out and said that the CDs on her shelf had moved. (This happened before we knew anything about Rosie.)

Yes, it really did happen. I always like to have everything in order and straight and the CDs weren't straight; each shelf was uneven.

It was when the medium was talking to me about Rosie, he said that she had been in the bedroom and had moved the CDs...

Now how on earth would he have known that? I said to him that I knew someone was in the room that night and that's why I couldn't go up. He replied; "I know you did, because you too have the same ability as I have."

He told me that I have seen people and although I told him that this was true I didn't want to talk about it. He said that I should do what he does and not waste my gift.

I simply said, "No!" and I refused to discuss the matter further. He was right but I have also seen several tragedies before they have actually happened and that's the reason I will not participate in any form of spiritualism.

Anyway, the medium told me that Rosie said she liked the tattoos that I had recently had done, but there was a debate about the colour. He said that she liked the colour and that I had made the right choice.

I was amazed at his accuracy. After seeing my medical records and realising that the medium had been right in everything he said, I went and had two further tattoos, one at each side of Jerry's name. A red rose and a red star.

The rose being Rosie and red because it is Chantelle's favourite colour. The star was because the medium described her as the brightest star in the sky, I was however going to have it in silver but had second thoughts and had got it in red too.

So it just goes to show, although I am skeptical about mediums there is, indeed, something out there that we don't, and perhaps never will, understand.

In all the readings I had, the mediums would tell me that my dad was there. I told them that my dad was very much alive but they kept saying, "No, he is here," and they kept giving me the name 'Tom, Tam or Tommy'. My real dad's name is, of course, Thomas.

I had also been told by the medium who told me about Rosie, that my brother was with me too. "My brother?" I questioned.

"Yes," he said.

I replied, "I don't think so, my brother is alive."

He said, "No, he is definitely your brother; he is calling you sis and he is the double of you."

"I'm not aware of a brother who has passed, unless he is my biological father's child?"

"He is saying his name is Steve," said the medium.

However, I don't know of a Steve; maybe he is or, rather, was a child of my dad.

It took a long, long time for me to get over the fact that the doctors had failed to tell us about Rosie and, after what has happened to me and my health, I doubt I will ever take what a doctor says as gospel that's for sure.

I didn't, and still haven't, told Jerry that while he was working overseas and the girls were at school there was many a day when I just cried over Rosie. I didn't want to put any stress on Jerry knowing that he was silently suffering too.

Chantelle will be going into sixth form at high school after this coming summer holiday, so for now we will have to keep quiet about Rosie. I have told Leanne, though, and my aunt and uncle, because if I hadn't I think I would have lost my mind by now.

15
Two Abodes

Talking of my aunt, I probably spent around half my life living with her and, as a young child, I pretty much went most places with her.

My uncle worked a nightshift and my aunt didn't like staying on her own and, although she had three children, they were very young.

This is the aunt I told you about who I would tell my friends was my big sister, silly now looking back but I didn't like being the oldest.

I loved staying with my aunt as she wasn't as strict as my parents but she did have her moments, like when I wrote a note to my PE teacher saying please excuse Belinda from PE as she is not well enough to participate.

Well, I sure didn't get away with that one because he called her to confirm that she wrote the letter. Did she say yes? Not a chance, she told him I had written it myself, so not only was I on report, I was grounded the whole week that I stayed with her.

I never did try anything like that again. My aunt wasn't strict in the sense that, at fifteen, she would send me to bed by eight o'clock at night like my parents – that was so embarrassing.

I have many fond memories of staying at my aunt's and of the times before she was married. She would invite me stay for weekends at the hotel where she worked in Arrochar, Scotland.

As a toddler she would take me whenever she was hanging out with her friends, that part I don't remember being as I was so young.

In fact, I don't really remember too much of my early childhood, although I do remember all the hidings I got.

There is a quote by Danu Grayson I remember from years ago that I used to say fitted me to a T, it was how I would have described myself back then…

'I'm quirky, silly, blunt and broken,

My days are sometimes dark,

My nights are sometimes long,

I often trip over my own insecurities,

I require attention, long for passion and

wish to be desired.

I use music to speak, when words fail me,

Even though the words are as important,

to me as the air I breathe.

I love hard, and with all that I have…

And even with my faults,

I am worth loving.'

It's funny how a simple quote, song or even an image can sum you up in one, yet no matter how powerful it reads, sounds or even looks, nobody sees it.

Everyone, and I have been guilty of this myself, can see faults in others but just one mistake leaves an impression so deep that they fail to see the good, or the heart within.

I've always said that our mistakes and wrongdoings are sent to try us, it's a learning curve and we can either sit and feel sorry for ourselves or pick ourselves up and get on with it. God knows I have paid the Pied Piper for my mistakes, but this last 20 years have been my best years and I wouldn't wish it to be any different.

Even beforehand when things were bad, I just picked myself up, dusted down and started again even though my heart was breaking.

16
Achievements

If someone was to ask me, what is the best thing that has happened to me, what have I achieved and learned up until now? I would simply say that my children are the best thing. Yes, there were times back when I was married before, that I thought I wouldn't have that bond back with Leanne and that I would not have any more children.

I firmly believe that it was all meant to be, because I have learned so much in the process. I have learned that, with love and determination, beautiful things can happen, and they can happen to us all.

Some people need to just sit back and breathe, ask themselves what they want out of life and go for it, because tomorrow isn't promised.

What are my personal achievements? I have many, for which I'm grateful, both in a working environment and my home life.

When I look back and think about the things that were good and bad in my life, there are more bad than good. I have had to cope with a lot of difficult times and I have mentioned some of these throughout my story, both here and in *Sad, Lonely & A Long Way From Home,* my first book.

I haven't, however, revealed all that has happened, some of the things in my life I can't seem to talk about without hurting all over again, both during my childhood and in teenage years.

Maybe, one day in the future, I will write another book or short story to tell all, but now is not the time for various reasons.

One reason is that I don't want to hurt the feelings of those who hurt me, I'm in a good place right now and don't need the rejection.

I was just sitting here thinking about the time I broke into a military training centre, back in Glasgow, when I was about eight going on nine maybe.

I was with friends, some of whom were older than me, and they came up with this idea that we could go and hang out in a building that they said was abandoned.

They climbed up a ladder to get in through the skylight window but, because I had my dog with me, I had to wait for them to get inside and open a door to let me in.

We had been in there quite some time before we heard voices at the other end of the building, so we all ran to escape.

I ran as fast as my little legs could take me and bolted out the door with my dog in tow. The others were all over the place; some came running out of the door and others jumped through the widow, but only my friends who were leaving via the window got caught.

Me, another friend and my dog got away and, at that time, we assumed that everyone had done so.

I went to the ice cream van some time later to buy cigarettes for my mum, only to turn around and see a friend being escorted by the police up the stairs to his house.

He saw me, pointed his finger, and said that I had been there too. Well, I was shaking in terror because I realised that I was in deep trouble. I gave my mum her cigarettes, ran into my room, put on my pyjamas and jumped into bed.

Next thing, the police were at the door. I could hear them talking to my mum and she was not best pleased.

The policeman came into my room, sat at the edge of my bed and asked me what I had stolen? "What!" I said, "I didn't steal anything, I was just looking around with my friends."

I looked towards the bedroom door where my mum was standing with a belt in her hand. She said to me "You're getting this when the policeman leaves."

I was petrified. The police officer then started to look under my bed and pillow, saying, "Come on, give me whatever it was that you stole."

I was, by this time, crying my heart out and said, "I didn't steal anything." Well, right there he slapped me across the face. Back then the police were allowed to give you a clip round the ear.

I looked at my mum because he had slapped me and she just stood there staring right through me, I knew then I was for another hiding. The thing is, I honestly can't remember if I did get a hiding that night or not because it happened frequently.

It wasn't the last time I was involved with the police either. When Michael, Leanne's father, and I were together I had a visit from them with regards to a stolen TV.

Michael had a Jaguar car, which I didn't like. I don't think they are pretty cars at all. However, he decided to sell it as we needed a van because, back then, we were market traders, so it made sense to have a van to transport our stock back and forth.

Someone I knew from years before (I went to school with his brother) had a transit van and said that he would like to do an exchange, but would also give us money to the value that we were selling the car.

I didn't have a good feeling about this guy but Michael thought he knew best and said that was a good deal.

To cut a long story short, he gave us the van, Michael gave him the car and, for weeks, we waited for the money, which I told Michael we would probably never see.

There were a lot of arguments back and forth going on about this money and, eventually, the guy gave Michael some of the cash. He also said that he would give him a colour TV for the rest, as he couldn't get the money together and Michael said that was fine.

It was a pretty smart TV. Back then, times were hard, to say the least, and we would never have been able to afford a TV like it.

However, I told Michael that I didn't trust this guy and thought he may have stolen the TV, as he wasn't the sort to be able to afford buying one.

Months later, Michael was down in London as by then we had expanded our trading to London. I was sitting watching TV, one morning, when there was a knock at the door. Leanne was a baby at the time.

It was the CID, I was stunned but, at the same time, had a feeling it was about that TV. The officers asked to come in and speak to me and I showed them in.

They said that a house had been broken into and a TV had been stolen. They had information that the TV was at our address. I was furious.

I showed them the TV that we had, they checked the serial number, and, sure as God, that was the one they were looking for.

I went on to tell them how we came about having the TV, only to be informed that it had been stolen from a house that an elderly lady had lived in.

By this time I was shaking with anger that an old lady had had this done to her. I told them the name of the man whom we had dealt with and they confirmed that he was the one that had broken into her home.

I then told them that I would make him pay for this. They said, "Well, you may have a long wait because he was charged a couple of weeks ago for another crime and is in Saughton Prison in Edinburgh."

I told them that I would wait on his release because I wasn't about to let it be forgotten. Needless to say, we weren't charged for receiving stolen goods because we had no idea that the TV had been stolen.

I did, however, get told off and they said that if I did what I said I was going to do to the man responsible when he came out of prison, I would be charged. (I won't tell you what I said I would do to him.)

The only time I had dealings with the police after that was when I was going through domestic violence with an ex-partner, Andrew.

17
Pondering Thoughts

I often sit and wonder what my life would have been like had I gone overseas as I planned to do. When I look back, I say, *If only I knew then what I know now.* Maybe I would have gone abroad many years before.

Although I went to live in Wales, it had crossed my mind to work and live overseas and sometimes, not often, I wish I had. If I thought back then that Jerry and I would not have met then maybe I would have gone but, like I say, my life has been mapped out for me.

Jerry and I did think of going to live overseas when the girls were babies. We had planned to go and live in Portugal as the girls would have started school at six but, unfortunately, we left it too late.

I still dream, even now, that maybe one day we can still up sticks and go, although time is running out as we are both fifty, so maybe not.

If I get my little cottage again then I'm happy enough to stay put, what is it they say? What's for you won't go by you.

They say that I'm a bit of a dreamer, that I talk too much, and sometimes too fast, and they are right, but it's good to dream. It is what keeps me going. I had so many dreams and aspirations when I was younger, some I fulfilled and others not, but maybe my girls will live my dreams or at least some of them.

Sinead is very like me and also talks too much, and we can get a little excited when we have conversation which very often has Jerry telling us to both shut up! All in fun, of course, and we love it.

I'm not sure how long Jerry will continue to work away from home. I do know that he is extremely happy that he was given the chance to fulfil his dream of working overseas and we are so proud of him and all he has achieved.

I've remembered something else; Jerry's ex-partner had gone to a medium many years ago and they told her that she and Jerry they wouldn't always be together.

They said that Jerry would end up dating someone he went to school with and even gave the initial of her name, and guess what? Here I am; they were spot on.

Jerry didn't have much faith in mediums either, but has since said there is obviously something in it after what we were told.

I always said that, one day, I would write a book and here I am on my second one. It won't be for everyone but I'm sure there will be many, especially those who know me, that will read my books and realise I'm not who they thought I was, and that includes family.

It's a learning curve too, because after this book I will be writing short fictional novels and poetry.

I love to talk so why not write? I have already started my first fictional story it's called *The Empty Swing*. I'm getting quite excited about it so, fingers crossed, I do it justice.

I have taken on many projects over the years and have had quite a few jobs; hairdressing, catering, working in the travel industry, sales and marketing, the list goes on…

Business marketing and training are what I enjoy the most. I first took a business course back in 1986/7 and loved it and, from there, I worked at various jobs, training employees.

Leanne and Chantelle both have that same business mind and are good at it so, all being well, they will eventually have a good career in that field.

Sinead is more technical and loves photography and filming. She hopes to be a director within the movie industry, and I firmly believe she can do it. She is a great script writer, and has produced and edited a short movie, so good luck to her.

As I have said before, I'm not sure where I would have been or what career path I would have chosen had everything been different but, in all honesty, I'm so glad I am where I am and with the people I love.

I was talking to a friend, not so long ago, who was going through so much she just didn't know where to turn. She, too, had been going through domestic violence and when she eventually got away from it, and talked about it, people would ask, "Why didn't you get away before now?"

Those individuals obviously don't know what it is like to be at the other end of a man's fist, nor have to put up with mental abuse.

I remember, years ago, my mum was watching a programme on television and the story was about a woman who was suffering terribly at the hands of her husband.

My mum said, "Why the hell doesn't she just pack her bags and go?"

I said to her, with a lump in my throat, "Mum, unless you have ever been in that situation don't sit there in judgement, you have no idea just what domestic abuse does to people."

She looked at me and asked, "How would you know?"

All I could say, whilst feeling quite sick, was "Well, if you had listened to me when I came back home to Scotland to live, then maybe you would understand."

I knew exactly what the woman in question was going through and I felt her pain, because it brought it all

110

back to me. I had only been back in Scotland less than a year at the time so it was still very raw.

People need to understand that myself, and others like me, didn't choose to live with a man who lifted their hand or tried to control us.

You meet a man and you fall in love but, let me assure you, he can turn out to be a very different man once the commitment is made, and not just after you're married. If you live with him, you soon come to see his true colours.

I've even come across couples who don't live together, who are just dating, and it happens. I will mention, too, that it's not always men who are the abusers, it can also be women.

I remember, on occasion when I was with Andrew, it would be so bad that I would sit on the corner of the settee too scared to move.

He would be there shouting and making threats, so much so that my eyelids would twitch with fear. I would think, *Look at me sat here like a little child scared to move.* I hated him so much.

What really hurt me was that the fact that I was a grown woman allowing this to happen, but what could I do?

On one occasion, he had a Stanley knife in his hand and fear took over. It didn't matter how many tears I shed that night, he still tried to slash my wrists and, by the grace of God, I managed to stop that knife slicing through my veins, although my hand caught the worst of it.

I still have the scar and when I look at it, which isn't often, it reminds me what a fool I was to have allowed him to control me the way he did.

Perhaps, if I had hit him back the first time he may have thought twice the next but, back then, I didn't think of it that way, because these men get into your head, they make you think it's your fault and that you have done something to deserve their anger.

18
The Hand That Fed Him

There's a saying; 'Don't bite the hand that feeds you'. We've all heard it right? Well that's exactly what they did to me...

I used to think: *Why would someone who is supposed to love me, treat me the way they do?* I soon realised it's due to their own insecurities.

Abusers have a limited range of behaviours and thinking patterns. The methods that abusers, both male and female, use to manipulate us are a natural part of their personalities. They have dysfunctional minds.

I learned how they think, and why, from doing a psychology course years ago. They will swear that events never occurred and that certain things were never said, but over time we begin to question our sanity.

I know I did, I used to think it was my fault and I think that stems from early childhood and being accused or blamed for silly things, or things that I didn't actually do.

I remember the first time I was hit by a partner I actually thought it was normal. He broke me down until I thought I was going insane, but the worst abuse for me was when I was with Andrew.

His threats to cultivate fear, anxiety and despair had me thinking, at one point, that I may as well not be here anymore. I know I was wrong to think like this, but I actually believed it was the only way out.

I am glad I didn't do anything silly though, sadly, not everyone is so fortunate and can get out before it's too late.

Andrew's behaviour damaged my self-esteem, self-confidence and my emotional and psychological well-being. I was constantly on edge, wondering how he was going to react at anything I did or wanted to do.

Living with a person who is unpredictable is difficult, stressful and nerve-racking and it caused me to have extreme anxiety. It contributed to my already failing health; I never had any sense of balance in my life.

I always remind my daughters, and always will, never to let a man lift his hand to them or mentally abuse them, and that there are ways that they, and we as parents, can remove them from the situation.

The first time it happens, I tell them, carry on as if everything is okay, then the minute he is away from the home, or they are away from the house, come straight to us and we will have it stopped quick smart.

I know that sounds easier said than done, because I've been there but, looking back, I should have disappeared the first time it happened.

They will tell you it won't happen again and make all sorts of promises. For everyone who reads this book, IT WILL HAPPEN AGAIN. If you stay and forgive them then, yes, it most certainly will happen again.

Self-worth is so vital to your happiness, if you don't feel good about yourself it's hard to feel good about anything else and, sometimes, all you have to do is forget how they make you feel, and remember what you deserve.

Believe in yourself.

19
Life Today

I'm on chapter nineteen and, by now, so many things have changed. My second youngest sister, who stopped talking to me eight years ago, is now speaking to me again, my sister just under me has some sort of hang-up because she isn't talking to me or, at least, is trying to keep her distance. What have I done? I have no idea.

My youngest brother is plodding along, trying to get his landscaping business up and running, my youngest sister, Jo, and her partner have taken up photography and boy have they taken some pretty amazing photos. She has also started a catering course at college so I wish her good luck with that.

My parents are still living in their little cocoon, nothing has changed there, although I am rather worried about my mum as she isn't looking too well at the moment.

Aunts, uncles and cousins are all living their lives and doing well and even though I don't seem to look much older, I certainly do feel it, what with so many nieces, nephews, great nieces and great nephews; what a handful!

Leanne continues to do well at college and has passed all her business and accounts exams. She is now on a higher level course and is still the manager of one of the departments in a superstore.

Chantelle is now working for a large organisation on an apprenticeship with a guaranteed position at the end with opportunities for her to work overseas in the future. Sinead is doing well in school and at college. She is looking forward to going to university, all being well, within the next couple of years.

Jerry is still working for United Nations. He spent five years in Jerusalem and me and our girls have been over there to see him. What an amazing city; absolutely beautiful, and then he did ten months in Gaza but, unfortunately, we were not able to visit him there.

He is now in Haiti, working on the rebuilding project after the earthquake. He loves it there, loves the people and is very content.

We have also discovered that Jerry, Rosanna and John have another brother, Stuart, whom we are fortunate is now in our lives and is a welcome addition to the family.

And me, I'm still writing. I have just finished my first book of poetry called *Tears On My Pillow* which I hope to publish in the next month or so. My third book *The*

Empty Swing (fiction) is coming in 2017 and I'm really excited about this one.

Here is a little introduction to *The Empty Swing*:

1972, London, England.

Elizabeth McDaid, aged 18, was working for 'The Times' newspaper.

Elizabeth came from humble beginnings, living in Simi Valley, USA, her father, a farmer's son, was originally from Donegal, Ireland, and her mother, a seamstress, left the US for London in 1964, when Elizabeth was just 10-years-old.

Elizabeth was a quiet girl and she felt that she didn't belong in London, even throughout her school years she was rather reserved. Her mother and father were very private people and very protective of her.

Of course, she had friends but her parents didn't allow her to mingle outside of school. Elizabeth had studied hard to get where she was, and she enjoyed her job, but it wasn't enough.

She always felt there were bigger and better things that she could be doing, and she had a yearning to travel.

Elizabeth had this empty feeling and a recurring dream, or what she thought was a dream, of her sitting on a swing as a child and someone else on a swing next to her, although she knew that there was someone on the other swing she never did see a face.

Elizabeth missed her home back in Simi Valley so, one day at dinner, she said to her parents that she wanted to go back home to Simi for a holiday to visit relatives. There was a look of shock on her parents' faces and they immediately said no.

They told her that there were no relatives left in Simi, which Elizabeth found rather strange, because she knew that her mother had been receiving letters from back home on a regular basis. However, she dropped the subject when she realised that the thought of her going back there seemed to upset them.

Then, four years later, Elizabeth decided again to tell her parents that she was going back. An opportunity had arisen at work that would take her to Calabasas to cover a story in relation to the Pumpkin Festival. Elizabeth figured, as she would be in the area, she may as well go back and relive some childhood memories.

Back in Simi, Elizabeth began to realise exactly why her parents hadn't wanted her to return and, God knows, they tried so hard to persuade her to decline the offer that her employers were so keen for her to take.

Once there she began to unravel the truth behind why they had left Simi: Did she stay or did she leave? And how did her parents explain the unusual, yet bizarre, set of circumstances that had led to them leaving the valley? And who was it on the other swing?

I'm quite excited about *The Empty Swing* because there is a twist in the story so I'm really keen to get it published as early as I can in 2017.

As for my book of poetry I started writing poems around the summer of 2016. I wrote my first poem called 'Father's Day Again' back in 2014 in memory of my father. I used to recite poetry as a youngster but didn't do anything with it for fear that I wouldn't be taken seriously.

However, after writing the poem for my father, I thought I would give it another go and see how it went. Some of my poems were read by family and friends, who said that they liked them, so I made up my mind to write a book of poetry.

Although it is called *Tears On My Pillow*, it's not all doom and gloom and, who knows, the title may change before it's published, although I doubt it. I wanted to write poems about personal circumstances I have been through that others would relate to who, perhaps, have had the same experiences but just can't find the words to express them.

20
Country Road

The road I travelled so many years ago is now a distant
memory, buried deep below.

The road I loved and miss so much is a picture now that I
can only touch.

Country road take me to that place, I don't want it to

become a haze, where water flows in the river below and

those coal fires with their glow, the warmth in winter

when the snow would fall and bread in the oven, enough
for us all.

Oh, how I miss those valleys with hills and trees as far as

the eye can see, where people came together on special
days.

I really don't want that to become a haze.

Cows in the field as I chopped the logs while the smell of

the coal was never blocked, lambing season the sound of

the sheep as they see their little ones carted off to the
jeep.

A country pub was my Saturday joint, meeting with

friends, drink in hand, while listening to the band.

Oh how I miss that band.

Sunday was best, my day of rest, woken to the sound of
the birds outside, sat on the coal bunker, those sounds
that told me of their hunger.
Sunday dinner in the oven a fine roast and all the
trimmings while humming to music which I found
therapeutic.
Trees that formed a tunnel when heavy snow lay above it
made me feel like I was wrapped inside a glove, that
image will remain with me forever.
What I would give to live in the country again, writing
books with my fancy pen, would I ever leave this time?
No never again.

~ Belinda Conniss

Acknowledgements

This book is dedicated to my husband, Jerry, our daughters Sherri-Leanne, Chantelle and Sinead, to our grandson, Damien, and granddaughters, Hayleigh and Hannah. My life would not have been complete without you.
I love you all.

To my mother, Isabella, who chose to bring me into this world when she was advised not to, for that I thank you.

I would like to thank Kim Kimber (www.kimkimber.co.uk), for copy-editing *Secrets & Lies* the sequel to *Sad, Lonely & A Long Way From home* which she also copy-edited, and for keeping me on track.

I would also like to thank Martin Sweeny of Knightshadesphotography.co.uk for the cover photograph

22987794R00074

Printed in Great Britain
by Amazon